PACKAGE YOUR GENIUS

COMPANION PERSONAL BRANDING WORKBOOK

ISBN:9781729219362

Copyright © 2018 Amanda Miller Littlejohn

All Rights Reserved.

No part of this book may be reproduced or utilized in any form or by any means, electronic or mechanical, including photocopying, recording, or by any information storage and retrieval system, without permission in writing from the author.

ABOUT THIS WORKBOOK

This workbook was developed by the author to serve as a companion to the book **Package Your Genius: 5 Steps to Build Your Most Powerful Personal Brand**. This workbook does not replace the book, but should be used in conjunction with the main text to capture your thoughts and help you create a plan of action. If you have not yet read the main text, you are encouraged to first acquire and read the main book before you attempt to use the workbook which was intended as a supplemental resource.

ACKNOWLEDGEMENTS

Thank you for everyone who supported the initial **Package Your Genius 5 Steps to Build Your Most Powerful Personal Brand** book project! Because of your feedback, this workbook is now a reality and new resource. Thank you for supporting the vision and offering the insights that made this workbook possible.

AMANDA MILLER LITTLEJOHN
Founder, *Package Your Genius Academy*

step one:

GET CLEAR ON YOUR BRAND

step one:
GET CLEAR ON YOUR BRAND

What if everyday you woke up and went to work doing something you loved? That is the case when you are operating in your zone of genius, when you have identified and leveraged your strengths. But what are your strengths?

What makes you feel strong?
What invigorates you and makes you feel as if you were born to do it?
What does the world mirror back to you?
What do people thank you for, and ask for your help with?

THESE ARE CLUES TO YOUR NATURAL STRENGTHS.

Remember as you work through this section: **ease is the way**. Too often, we mistakenly think that work has to be difficult to be worthwhile, but on the contrary our strengths come so easy to us because we were born to do them. What comes easy for you but is difficult for others?

BE WILLING TO GO BACK IN TIME AND LOOK FOR CHILDHOOD CLUES.

Our core strengths often emerge in childhood. Think back to yourself at age 8, 9, or 10. What would your 10 year old self do for fun? What would the 10 year old you get excited about? What was he or she good at?

FINALLY, LOOK BACK ON THE YEAR BEHIND YOU AND THINK ABOUT YOUR HIGHLIGHT REEL.

When were your moments of absolute bliss — especially at work? What made you feel like you were doing what you were meant to do? Let's go after more of that.

Use the questions of this section to help you get closer to a clear vision of who you are and what you were born to do.

face your genius:
GET IN TOUCH WITH YOUR CHILDHOOD SELF

WHAT DID YOU DO FOR FUN AS A CHILD WHEN YOU HAD NO ONE DIRECTING YOUR TIME?

WHAT WERE SOME OF YOUR CHILDHOOD PASSIONS? WHERE DID YOU EXCEL? WHICH ACTIVITIES DID YOU ENJOY MOST?

Personal Branding Companion Workbook

face your genius:

GET IN TOUCH WITH YOUR CHILDHOOD SELF

WHAT VALUABLE WORK DO YOU CURRENTLY REFUSE TO CHARGE FOR, OR FEEL GUILTY CHARGING FOR?

WHERE DO YOU RELAX AND LEAN INTO BEING THAT YOU DON'T EVEN REMEMBER WHAT YOU'RE DOING?

face your genius:
GET IN TOUCH WITH YOUR CHILDHOOD SELF

WHAT WORK DO OTHERS SEEM TO COMPLIMENT YOU ON THE MOST?

WHAT WORK FEELS EFFORTLESS FOR YOU, BUT IS CLEARLY DIFFICULT FOR OTHERS?

clarify your genius:
GET IN TOUCH WITH YOUR CHILDHOOD SELF

IDENTIFY YOUR STRENGTHS, SKILLS, AND THE VALUE YOU PROVIDE

WHAT ARE YOUR MOST DOMINANT TECHNICAL SKILLS? SOFT SKILLS?

Package Your Genius

clarify your genius:
GET IN TOUCH WITH YOUR CHILDHOOD SELF

> WHEN YOU THINK OF YOUR LIFE'S MISSION, WHAT AUDIENCES ARE YOU DRAWN TO HELP, SUPPORT, OR SERVE?

> WHAT IS YOUR IDEAL MODE OF WORKING? DO YOU PREFER WORKING ALONE, WORKING ON TEAMS, SPEAKING ON STAGES, WRITING OUT YOUR IDEAS, ETC.?

Personal Branding Companion Workbook

clarify your genius:
GET IN TOUCH WITH YOUR CHILDHOOD SELF

WHEN DO YOU FEEL ENERGIZED? WHAT WORK ARE YOU DOING WHEN YOU FEEL MOST ENERGIZED?

WHAT HAVE BEEN SOME OF YOUR "PEAK MOMENTS"?

clarify your genius:
GET IN TOUCH WITH YOUR CHILDHOOD SELF

WHAT DO PEOPLE THANK YOU FOR?

WHAT DO PEOPLE TEND TO ASK FOR YOUR HELP WITH?

Personal Branding Companion Workbook

clarify your genius:

GET IN TOUCH WITH YOUR CHILDHOOD SELF

> ARE YOU CURRENTLY "STEERING YOUR OWN SHIP"? IF NOT, WHOSE OPINIONS GUIDE THE DECISIONS YOU MAKE FOR YOUR LIFE AND/OR CAREER?

> WHAT IS YOUR VISION FOR YOUR GIFTS AND TALENTS? IF SUCCESS WERE GUARANTEED, WHAT WOULD YOU BE DOING? WHY AREN'T YOU DOING THAT NOW?

clarify your genius:
GET IN TOUCH WITH YOUR CHILDHOOD SELF

WHEN IN THE PAST HAVE YOU FOUND YOURSELF WORKING TOWARDS SOMEONE ELSE'S VISION FOR YOUR GIFTS AND TALENTS? JOURNAL ABOUT THAT BELOW.

communicate your genius:

PACKAGE A BRAND MESSAGE THAT CONNECTS

WHAT IS YOUR SOLUTION? WHAT PROBLEMS DO YOU SOLVE?

WHAT AUDIENCE NEEDS THE PROBLEM YOU SOLVE? WHAT SITUATION ARE PEOPLE TYPICALLY IN WHEN THEY REACH OUT TO YOU?

WHO NATURALLY GRAVITATES TO YOU AND REQUESTS YOUR HELP? WHO TYPICALLY REQUESTS YOUR SOLUTION?

communicate your genius:
PACKAGE A BRAND MESSAGE THAT CONNECTS

WHAT WORKING ENVIRONMENT AND FORMAT USUALLY BRINGS OUT YOUR BEST?

WHICH PEOPLE DO YOU FIND EASY, EFFORTLESS, AND ENERGIZING TO HELP?

Personal Branding Companion Workbook

communicate your genius:

PACKAGE A BRAND MESSAGE THAT CONNECTS

WHAT IS YOUR NARRATIVE? COMBINE THE PROBLEM YOU SOLVE + THE AUDIENCE YOU HELP + THE SOLUTION PEOPLE ARE IN BEFORE THEY COME TO YOU INTO A BRAND NARRATIVE BELOW.

step two:

MAKE THE CASE

communicate your genius:

PACKAGE A BRAND MESSAGE THAT CONNECTS

In many instances, how you've done what you've done is as important as what you've achieved. Beyond your technical skills, you'll that find your transferrable and soft skills are your "secret sauce" and the basis for your professional reputation as your career progresses. What terms can you make it your business to become known for? Circle the terms that speak to your current professional reputation. Which words and phrases can you weave into your narrative as you make the case for new opportunities? Use these words and phrases as a starting point and brainstorm a few of your own in the back of the workbook, before moving on to the next set of questions.

DEPENDABLE

COLLABORATIVE

FLAWLESS PRODUCT - FEW MISTAKES

THOROUGH

RESOURCEFUL

INTELLECTUALLY CURIOUS

STRONG EXECUTION SKILLS

STRONG, NATURAL LEADER

INSIGHTFUL

THINKS AHEAD

TIMELY

CREATIVE THINKER

GETS PROJECTS "UNSTUCK"

DIPLOMATIC

IS SO EASY TO WORK WITH

GREAT COMMUNICATOR

STRONG PROJECT MANAGEMENT SKILLS

MOTIVATING TEAM MEMBER

FUN TO BE AROUND

BUILDS A TEAM

FINISHES WHAT HE STARTS

SELF-MOTIVATED, SELF STARTER

Package Your Genius

receipts:
SHOWCASE EVIDENCE OF YOUR WORK AND VALUE

WHAT STELLAR RESULTS HAVE YOU ACHIEVED DURING THE COURSE OF YOUR CAREER?

WHAT ARE 3-5 SPECIFIC PAST WORK EXPERIENCES YOU CAN DEVELOP CASE STUDIES AROUND?

Personal Branding Companion Workbook

receipts:
SHOWCASE EVIDENCE OF YOUR WORK AND VALUE

WHOM HAVE YOU DONE GREAT WORK FOR IN THE PAST?

HOW CAN YOU USE YOUR PAST EVIDENCE TO MAKE THE CASE FOR SOMETHING NEW?

receipts:
SHOWCASE EVIDENCE OF YOUR WORK AND VALUE

> WHAT EVIDENCE AND CASE STUDIES CAN YOU EXTRACT FROM THOSE YOU WORKED WELL WITH?

> WHAT EVIDENCE DO YOU NEED TO MAKE THE CASE FOR A NEW POSITION? HOW WILL YOU GO ABOUT GETTING THE EVIDENCE YOU NEED?

Personal Branding Companion Workbook

receipts:
SHOWCASE EVIDENCE OF YOUR WORK AND VALUE

WHAT DOES YOUR CURRENT EVIDENCE SAY ABOUT YOUR CAPABILITIES? WHAT STORY DOES IT TELL?

HOW DOES THE STORY YOU'RE TELLING THROUGH YOUR CURRENT EVIDENCE ALIGN WITH YOUR ULTIMATE CAREER GOALS?

let others talk:
SECURE INVALUABLE SOCIAL PROOF

WHO ARE SOME OF YOUR MOST ENTHUSIASTIC BRAND OR CAREER CHAMPIONS?

WHO HOLDS YOU IN HIGH REGARD AND REGULARLY SPEAKS IN GLOWING TERMS ABOUT YOU?

Personal Branding Companion Workbook

let others talk:
SECURE INVALUABLE SOCIAL PROOF

LIST THE COLLEAGUES WHO CAN ENTHUSIASTICALLY RECOMMEND YOUR WORK AS WELL AS WHAT WORK YOU WANT THEM TO REFERENCE. REQUEST RECOMMENDATIONS ON LINKEDIN.

WHO CAN SPEAK TO THE CONTRIBUTION YOU ARE CAPABLE OF MAKING TO ANOTHER ORGANIZATION?

let others talk:
SECURE INVALUABLE SOCIAL PROOF

― LIST THE WORK AND PROJECTS YOU NEED TO SECURE RECOMMENDATIONS FOR. ―

― WHAT DO YOU WANT MORE OF? I.E. MORE HIGH-END CLIENTS, MORE SPEAKING ENGAGEMENTS, MORE BOOK SALES - WHAT SOCIAL PROOF DO YOU NEED TO GO AFTER TO HELP YOU MAKE THE CASE? ―

Personal Branding Companion Workbook

let others talk:
SECURE INVALUABLE SOCIAL PROOF

WHAT MENTORS, MENTEES, OR PAST CLIENTS CAN YOU APPROACH FOR RECOMMENDATIONS/TESTIMONIALS?

WHAT TECHNICAL SKILLS CAN YOU SECURE RECOMMENDATIONS FOR?

let others talk:
SECURE INVALUABLE SOCIAL PROOF

WHAT SOFT SKILLS CAN YOU PLAY UP IN YOUR CONVERSATIONS ABOUT YOURSELF? WHAT SOFT SKILLS WOULD OTHERS BE WILLING TO COMMENT ON AND ENDORSE TO CREATE SOCIAL PROOF ONLINE?

Personal Branding Companion Workbook

let others talk:
SECURE INVALUABLE SOCIAL PROOF

IF RELEVANT, WHERE CAN YOU SECURE RATINGS OR REVIEWS? WHOM CAN YOU SOLICIT?

step three:

DEFINE YOUR BIG IDEAS

Your big ideas form the basis of the most memorable parts of your personal brand platform. When I use the term "big ideas," I mean the thought leadership content that has the power to set you apart from others in your industry. Author Tara Mohr's book "Playing Big" or psychologist Brene Brown's book and platform "Daring Greatly" are both examples of big ideas that have been expanded into books or contracted into other formats like media articles and Ted talks. Where can you find your own big ideas?

Use the story prompts below to help you remember some of the most pivotal and powerful points in your life. Pick 2-3 to journal about on the following pages. The prompts will likely also help you answer the questions in this section. Make note of the connections.

YOUR FIRST MEMORY OF BECOMING FRUSTRATED BY THE PROBLEM YOU HOPE TO SOLVE

YOUR FIRST MEMORY OF BEING ENERGIZED BY YOUR WORK

A PERSON WHO YOU WILL NEVER FORGET AND WHY

A MAJOR MOMENT FROM CHILDHOOD THAT CHANGED YOU. WHAT LESSON DID YOU LEARN?

A MAJOR CAREER MOMENT THAT CHANGED YOU. HOW DID IT CHANGE YOU? WHAT LESSONS DID YOU LEARN?

A TIME YOU MADE A BIG MISTAKE/SOMETHING YOU'LL NEVER DO AGAIN

A MOMENT YOU DIDN'T TRUST YOUR GUT AND WENT ON TO REGRET IT

A TIME YOU WERE BRAVE

WHEN YOU HAD TO MAKE A TOUGH DECISION

A TIME YOU TURNED THINGS AROUND AT WORK

A TIME YOU TURNED THINGS AROUND IN YOUR PERSONAL LIFE

THE MOMENT YOU KNEW YOU WERE NO LONGER HAPPY

THE MOMENT YOU KNEW FOR SURE

SOMETHING YOU COULD NEVER TAKE BACK

THE MOMENT YOU REALIZED YOU DIDN'T WANT OTHERS TO FACE A PARTICULAR CHALLENGE (OR GO THROUGH WHAT YOU WENT THROUGH)

YOUR STORIES

YOUR STORIES

what to share:
UNCOVER YOUR THOUGHT LEADERSHIP

WHAT DO YOU KNOW A LOT ABOUT - MORE THAN THE AVERAGE PERSON IN YOUR FIELD?

WHAT IS YOUR CORE PROBLEM-SOLVING MESSAGE? WHAT HELPFUL INFORMATION DO YOU WAN THE WORLD TO KNOW?

Personal Branding Companion Workbook

what to share:
UNCOVER YOUR THOUGHT LEADERSHIP

WHAT ADVICE DO PEOPLE CONSISTENTLY THANK YOU FOR? HOW WOULD YOU DELIVER IT IN A STEP BY STEP OR LISTICLE FORMAT?

WHAT FREQUENTLY ASKED QUESTIONS DO YOU FIND YOURSELF ANSWERING OFTEN? HOW COULD YOU USE THOSE QUESTIONS TO CREATE HELPFUL WRITTEN, AUDIO, OR VIDEO CONTENT?

what to share:
UNCOVER YOUR THOUGHT LEADERSHIP

> WHEN YOU THINK OF THE PROBLEMS YOU SEE MOST OFTEN, WHAT IS YOUR STEP BY STEP PRESCRIPTION FOR CHANGE? COULD THIS FORM THE BASIS OF A BOOK OR COURSE?

> WHAT ARE THE STEPS OF THIS PRESCRIPTION? WHAT ORDER SHOULD THEY BE COMPLETED IN? COULD THESE STEPS BE BOOK CHAPTERS OR COURSE MODULES?

Personal Branding Companion Workbook

how to share:
DEVELOP A PERSONAL CONTENT STRATEGY

WHAT GOALS WILL YOUR CONTENT HELP YOU ACCOMPLISH? I.E. SELL MORE SERVICES, RAISE YOUR PROFILE, HELP YOU LAND A BOARD SEAT.

WHAT IS YOUR BIG IDEA? WHAT'S ONE BIG UMBRELLA TOPIC (I.E. PACKAGE YOUR GENIUS) YOU CAN DEVELOP MANY THOUGHT LEADERSHIP MINI-TOPICS UNDER (I.E. PACKAGE YOUR GENIUS FOR PR)?

how to share:
DEVELOP A PERSONAL CONTENT STRATEGY

WHAT IS YOUR MISSION? WHY DID YOU BEGIN DOING THE WORK YOU ARE CURRENTLY DOING?

WHAT FORMATS WILL YOU USE TO DEVELOP CONTENT? AUDIO? VIDEO? WRITING?

Personal Branding Companion Workbook

how to share:
DEVELOP A PERSONAL CONTENT STRATEGY

WHAT TOPICS ARE YOU ALREADY MOTIVATED TO SPEAK ABOUT?

WHAT TOPIC COULD ILLUSTRATE YOUR PASSION AND EXPERTISE TODAY?

how to share:
DEVELOP A PERSONAL CONTENT STRATEGY

WHAT CURRENT EVENTS OR INDUSTRY NEWS CAN YOU COMMENT ON RIGHT NOW?

WHAT CONVERSATIONS DO YOU WANT TO BE A PART OF? WHAT CONVERSATIONS ARE MISSING A UNIQUE PERSPECTIVE LIKE YOURS?

Personal Branding Companion Workbook

how to share:
DEVELOP A PERSONAL CONTENT STRATEGY

WHAT COMMON MISTAKES CAN YOU HIGHLIGHT THE ANSWERS TO?

LIST 10 PEOPLE WHOM YOU CAN PROFILE OR CONDUCT A Q&A SESSION WITH TO ALIGN YOUR BRAND MORE CLOSELY WITH YOUR AREA OF EXPERTISE.

how to share:
DEVELOP A PERSONAL CONTENT STRATEGY

WHAT IS YOUR PHILOSOPHY? WHAT GUIDES YOUR APPROACH TO YOUR WORK?

WHAT AUDIENCE(S) DO YOU CARE ABOUT THE MOST? WHAT GROUPS HAVE YOU ALWAYS WANTED TO IMPACT?

how to share:
DEVELOP A PERSONAL CONTENT STRATEGY

WHAT IS A STRETCH GOAL FOR YOUR CONTENT? COULD YOU SEE YOURSELF WRITING A BOOK, LAUNCHING YOUR OWN PODCAST OR PLANNING A CONFERENCE IN THE NEXT YEAR?

WHICH MEDIUM WILL YOU USE TO BEGIN PUBLISHING YOUR NEW CONTENT?

ideas to income:
MONETIZE YOUR BRAND THROUGH SIGNATURES

WHAT TOPIC OR TOPICS COULD YOU BUILD A SIGNATURE OFFER AROUND?

WHAT SOLID PIECE OF INSTRUCTIONAL CONTENT COULD YOU DEVELOP AND POTENTIALLY EXPAND INTO A LARGER PAID OFFERING?

ideas to income:

MONETIZE YOUR BRAND THROUGH SIGNATURES

WHAT SPEAKING PRESENTATION DECK COULD YOU REPURPOSE INTO A PAID WEBINAR, MASTERCLASS OR ONLINE COURSE?

WHAT NETWORK OF PEOPLE COULD YOU BRING TOGETHER FOR A LIVE EVENT? AROUND WHAT TOPIC?

ideas to income:
MONETIZE YOUR BRAND THROUGH SIGNATURES

WHAT FEATURED SPEAKERS WOULD YOU LIKE TO SEE? WHO IN YOUR NETWORK WOULD OTHER PEOPLE PAY TO SEE?

WHAT'S YOUR STYLE? WHAT IS THE MOST COMFORTABLE WAY FOR YOU TO DELIVER YOUR BEST RESULTS?

ideas to income:

MONETIZE YOUR BRAND THROUGH SIGNATURES

LIST THE PAID FORMATS YOU'D LIKE TO TRY. NETWORKING EVENT? CONSULTING PACKAGE? ONLINE COURSE? COACHING SESSION/PROGRAM? WHAT PROBLEM WOULD EACH FORMAT SOLVE?

WHEN CAN YOU REALISTICALLY INTRODUCE YOUR FIRST NEW SIGNATURE TO YOUR CURRENT AUDIENCE?

WHAT PATH HAVE YOU ALWAYS WANTED TO EXPLORE BUT HAVEN'T YET HAD THE COURAGE TO?

pivot:
REROUTE YOUR PATH WHEN THE TIME COMES

WHAT NEW AREA DO PEOPLE ASK FOR YOUR SUPPORT AROUND?

WHAT SERVICE DO OTHERS REQUEST FROM YOU THAT YOU DON'T CURRENTLY OFFER OR CHARGE FOR?

pivot:
REROUTE YOUR PATH WHEN THE TIME COMES

IF YOU COULD TRY ANYTHING RIGHT NOW, AND BE GUARANTEED SUCCESS, WHAT WOULD THAT THING BE?

IF YOU'RE CURRENTLY UNFULFILLED ON YOUR PATH, DO YOU WAN TO CHANGE YOUR INDUSTRY, YOUR TASKS, OR THE FOCUS OF YOUR IMPACT?

WHAT IS ONE SMALL CHANGE YOU CAN MAKE TO TEST THE WATERS OF A NEW DIRECTION?

step four:
MAKE YOURSELF VISIBLE

step four:
MAKE YOURSELF VISIBLE

In today's economy, whether you are employed by a company or you own your own company, the competition is fierce. To be on the short list of people who come to mind when key opportunities arise, you have to stand out. And in order to do so and become top of mind for decision makers, you must be prepared to make yourself known.

Yet there are simple ways to make yourself visible even if you're not ready to do a major media interview. Look through the list of ways to attract visibility and make note of the tactics you are willing to try, before you move on to answer the questions in this section.

COMMON WAYS TO INCREASE YOUR VISIBILITY

IN THE WORKPLACE
Speak up in meetings and on conference calls - make a point, or ask a question
Take on a project on another team
Schedule coffee meetings for face time

IN WRITING
Send an email update to your contacts
Write a guest post for an industry publication or major news site
Write a book

SPEAKING AND EVENTS
Speak on a panel
Submit to present at a conference
Apply to deliver a Ted Talk
Stand up and ask a question at a conference

ONLINE
Update your headshot on LinkedIn
Use hashtags to aid in search
Update your LinkedIn status
Take and post photos with influencers

MEDIA AND CONTENT
Request nomination for an award
Start your own blog, podcast or other content project
Get profiled in a major magazine's website
Book yourself as a podcast guest
Pitch yourself for a local television segment

OTHER
Serve on a board of directors

tap into social media:
LEVERAGE ONLINE TOOLS AND YOUR DIGITAL PRESENCE

> WHAT GOALS WILL SOCIAL MEDIA HELP YOU ACCOMPLISH? I.E. SELL MORE SERVICES, RAISE YOUR PROFILE, HELP YOU LAND A BOARD SEAT.

> WHOM DO YOU NEED TO REACH IN ORDER TO REACH YOUR PERSONAL BRAND GOALS? WHERE DOES THIS AUDIENCE HANG OUT ONLINE?

Personal Branding Companion Workbook

tap into social media:
LEVERAGE ONLINE TOOLS AND YOUR DIGITAL PRESENCE

> **WHAT PLATFORMS (3 MAX) WILL YOU FOCUS ON INITIALLY TO HELP YOU BUILD YOUR PERSONAL BRAND?**

> **WHAT MEDIA - SHORT TEXT/LONG FORM TEXT/PHOTO/VIDEO - MAKES THE MOST SENSE FOR YOUR SKILLS AND PERSONAL BRAND?**

tap into social media:
LEVERAGE ONLINE TOOLS AND YOUR DIGITAL PRESENCE

WHAT IS ONE GOAL YOU HAVE FOR SOCIAL MEDIA THAT YOU CAN WORK ON OVER THE NEXT THREE MONTHS?

LIST THE TOOLS YOU WILL USE TO MAKE THE WORK EASIER.

Personal Branding Companion Workbook

make your pitch:
PACKAGE YOUR IDEAS FOR THE MEDIA

WHAT ARE SOME OF YOUR MEDIA WORTHY PERSONAL OR PROFESSIONAL STORIES?

LIST YOUR 4 MOST NEWSWORTHY TIMES OF THE YEAR.

make your pitch:
PACKAGE YOUR IDEAS FOR THE MEDIA

WHICH PART OF YOUR EXPERTISE COULD BE PACKAGED FOR A LONGER (20-60 MIN) MEDIA SEGMENT?

WHAT TOPICS COULD YOU CONFIDENTLY GIVE A QUOTE ON?

Personal Branding Companion Workbook

make your pitch:
PACKAGE YOUR IDEAS FOR THE MEDIA

WHAT PUBLICATIONS EXIST FOR YOUR INDUSTRY?

LIST YOUR 4 MOST NEWSWORTHY TIMES OF THE YEAR.

make your pitch:
PACKAGE YOUR IDEAS FOR THE MEDIA

WHAT JOURNALISTS COULD BE ADDED TO YOUR MEDIA LIST?

WHAT PROGRAMS HAVE YOU WATCHED THAT SEEMED LIKE A GOOD OPPORTUNITY – EVEN IF THEY WERE A LONG SHOT FOR YOU?

Personal Branding Companion Workbook

make your pitch:
PACKAGE YOUR IDEAS FOR THE MEDIA

WHAT IS ONE TELEVISION OR ONLINE MEDIA OPPORTUNITY THAT YOU THINK YOU CAN SECURE WITHIN THE NEXT MONTH?

WHAT IS ONE LONGER LEAD MEDIA OPPORTUNITY YOU THINK YOU CAN SECURE IN THE NEXT SIX MONTHS?

find your stage:
PACKAGE YOUR IDEAS FOR PUBLIC SPEAKING

WHAT TOPIC CAN YOU DELIVER A SOLID 30-45 MINUTE PRESENTATION ON? OUTLINE YOUR POINTS BELOW.

WHAT IS ONE CALL FOR SPEAKERS YOU CAN SUBMIT/APPLY FOR?

Personal Branding Companion Workbook

find your stage:
PACKAGE YOUR IDEAS FOR PUBLIC SPEAKING

LIST THE UPCOMING CONFERENCES OR CONVENTIONS YOU'D LIKE TO OFFER YOUR TALENTS AS A SPEAKER.

WHAT COLLEGE OR UNIVERSITY STAGES WOULD YOU LIKE TO GRACE?

Package Your Genius

find your stage:
PACKAGE YOUR IDEAS FOR PUBLIC SPEAKING

NAME 3-5 CORPORATIONS THAT MAY NEED YOUR SPEAKING OR TRAINING EXPERTISE. IDENTIFY A POINT OF CONTACT FOR EACH ON LINKEDIN.

WHAT CHURCHES OR OTHER RELIGIOUS CONGREGATIONS MAY HAVE A SPEAKING OPPORTUNITY FOR YOU?

Personal Branding Companion Workbook

find your stage:
PACKAGE YOUR IDEAS FOR PUBLIC SPEAKING

RESEARCH 3-5 UPCOMING PANEL PRESENTATIONS YOU COULD YOU BE A GOOD FIT FOR. LIST BELOW.

WHAT SOLUTION-ORIENTED TOPIC COULD YOU DEVELOP A SOLID BREAKOUT SESSION AROUND?

find your stage:
PACKAGE YOUR IDEAS FOR PUBLIC SPEAKING

> WHAT WEBINAR OPPORTUNITIES EXIST FOR YOU TO PRESENT? WHAT WEBINAR TOPIC COULD YOU PRESENT ON FOR ANOTHER ORGANIZATION OR ON BEHALF OF YOURSELF?

> WHAT PROGRAMS HAVE YOU WATCHED THAT SEEMED LIKE A GOOD OPPORTUNITY - EVEN IF THEY WERE A LONG SHOT FOR YOU?

Personal Branding Companion Workbook

who knows you:
BE INTENTIONAL ABOUT YOUR NETWORK

RESEARCH AND LIST 5 NETWORKING EVENT YOU CAN ATTEND TO MEET YOUR TARGET AUDIENCE.

RESEARCH AND LIST 5 INDUSTRY AWARDS TO APPLY OR OBTAIN A NOMINATION FOR.

who knows you:
BE INTENTIONAL ABOUT YOUR NETWORK

WHO IS IN YOUR TRIBE NOW? WHAT RELATIONSHIPS ARE ALREADY SUPPORTIVE?

WHO IN YOUR LIFE SHOULD YOU PUT SOME DISTANCE BETWEEN WHILE YOU'RE IN THE FRAGILE STAGE OF GETTING YOUR BRAND OFF THE GROUND?

Personal Branding Companion Workbook

who knows you:
BE INTENTIONAL ABOUT YOUR NETWORK

> HOW CAN YOU NURTURE YOUR MOST SUPPORTIVE RELATIONSHIPS AND BE MORE INTENTIONAL ABOUT THE TIME YOU SPEND WITH THOSE PEOPLE? LIST 3 WAYS YOU'LL BE MORE INTENTIONAL.

> WHAT EVENTS ARE HAPPENING IN YOUR LOCAL AREA WHERE YOU CAN ATTEND AND GROW YOUR NETWORK? RESEARCH AND LIST 3-5 EVENTS.

who knows you:
BE INTENTIONAL ABOUT YOUR NETWORK

WHAT KEY EVENTS CAN YOU PLAN TO ATTEND IN OTHER CITIES, STATES, OR COUNTRIES TO MEET AND GROW YOUR IDEAL NETWORK?

WHAT INFLUENCERS DO YOU FOLLOW ONLINE? WHAT EVENTS DO THEY HOST? HOW CAN YOU GET INVOLVED?

Personal Branding Companion Workbook

who knows you:
BE INTENTIONAL ABOUT YOUR NETWORK

WHAT COMMUNITY CAN YOU CONVENE? WHAT EVENT CAN YOU HOST?

WHAT TOPIC OR PROBLEM CAN YOU START AN ONLINE COMMUNITY AROUND?

who knows you:
BE INTENTIONAL ABOUT YOUR NETWORK

WHAT MEET-UP, NETWORKING OR OTHER EVENT CAN YOU HOST TO BUILD COMMUNITY? WHAT AUDIENCE CAN YOU BRING TOGETHER?

WHERE MIGHT YOU FIND LIKE-MINDED PEOPLE TO GROW YOUR TRIBE? BRAINSTORM 3 NEW PLACES.

Personal Branding Companion Workbook

who knows you:

BE INTENTIONAL ABOUT YOUR NETWORK

NOTES

step five:
SELL YOURSELF

step five:
SELL YOURSELF

Ranking closely to public speaking, sales is one of the least favorite professional activities for many people, and for good reason. But one reframe I've used over the years is to simply think of selling as the opportunity to start a conversation with someone who has the problem you solve. In this way, you aren't asking for something. Instead, you're helping connect them to a resource they already need.

ANOTHER WAY TO THINK OF SELLING YOURSELF IS "CLOSING THE DEAL."

Think about it: why do the hard work of putting yourself out there as a thought leader, developing good content and extracting your big ideas if you're unwilling to close the deal?

It's up to you to not only identify opportunities to share your ideas, but also pitch yourself to the media or to event organizers as an expert.

It's up to you to not only revise your bio and LinkedIn profile with your accomplishments, but also share the full picture of those accomplishments in person when you sit down for a job interview.

It's up to you to not only outline a new paid consulting or coaching service, but also invite people to learn about it and potentially buy it!

IT'S UP TO YOU!

It's really difficult to sell a secret, so if you're committed to creating opportunities from your personal brand (not just attention and noise), understand that at some point you will have to invite others to potentially reject you when you put them in the position to say yes or no to what you have to offer. But the good news is, you have a 50/50 chance of getting a yes, and those are pretty good odds.

As I share at length in the main text, many people at this point in the process struggle with imposter syndrome and have a hard time promoting themselves with conviction. It's heartbreaking to watch them stop short, just yards from the proverbial finish line, as they begin to sabotage their own success.

Be forewarned of the ways this issue can crop up for high achievers, and use the journaling prompts to do the necessary introspection. Use the planning questions from this section of the workbook to assess your resources, understand your network, and create actionable steps to reach your goals.

be proactive:
INTENTIONALLY DEVELOP OPPORTUNITIES

> LIST TEN TARGET PEOPLE OR COMPANIES YOU'D LIKE TO WORK WITH OR FOR. HOW AND WHEN WILL YOU REACH OUT TO THEM?

> LIST A SPECIFIC POINT OF CONTACT FOR EACH TARGET ON YOUR LIST. USE COMPANY WEBSITES AND LINKEDIN TO FIND CONTACT INFORMATION.

Personal Branding Companion Workbook

be proactive:
INTENTIONALLY DEVELOP OPPORTUNITIES

WHAT AUDIENCES ARE TYPICALLY DRAWN TO YOU? LIST THEM BELOW.

RESEARCH AND LIST THE EVENTS WHERE CAN YOU NETWORK TO MEET THIS AUDIENCE EN MASSE.

be proactive:
INTENTIONALLY DEVELOP OPPORTUNITIES

> **WHO CAN REFER YOU TO MEMBERS OF THEIR NETWORK WHO MAY NEED WHAT YOU DO? MAKE A LIST OF 10 OR MORE POTENTIAL PARTNERS IN YOUR SUCCESS.**

> **WHO CAN INTRODUCE YOU TO NEW NETWORKS THAT YOU AREN'T ALREADY A PART OF?**

Personal Branding Companion Workbook

be proactive:
INTENTIONALLY DEVELOP OPPORTUNITIES

WHAT UPCOMING EVENTS CAN YOU ATTEND TO EXPAND YOUR NETWORK AND DEVELOP NEW MUTUALLY BENEFICIAL RELATIONSHIPS?

WHAT NEW INDUSTRIES OR SECTORS WILL YOU TARGET ORDER TO IDENTIFY NEW CLIENTS OR JOB PROSPECTS? LIST THE INDUSTRIES THAT FIT YOUR PERSONAL BRAND AND GOALS BELOW.

be proactive:
INTENTIONALLY DEVELOP OPPORTUNITIES

WHAT STALE LEADS AND DORMANT CONTACTS CAN YOU RE-ENERGIZE? WHAT PEOPLE FROM YOUR PAST HAVEN'T YOU SEEN IN SOME TIME? LIST AT LEAST 10 PEOPLE YOU CAN FOLLOW UP WITH.

WHAT 90-120 MIN WINDOW EACH WEEK CAN YOU DEVOTE TO OPPORTUNITY DEVELOPMENT (PITCHING THE MEDIA, CONDUCTING DISCOVERY SESSIONS AND SALES CALLS, FOLLOWING UP ON LEADS)? PLUG THIS TIME IN YOUR CALENDAR AS A RECURRING MEETING WITH YOURSELF.

Personal Branding Companion Workbook

master your time:
TRAIN YOURSELF TO BE PRODUCTIVE

WHAT 3 GOALS DO WANT TO ACCOMPLISH IN THE NEXT 90 DAYS? THE NEXT YEAR? WHERE ARE YOU REGULARLY ALLOCATING TIME FOR THOSE GOALS IN YOUR SCHEDULE?

HOW COULD YOU BETTER ALIGN YOUR USE OF TIME WITH YOUR GOALS?

master your time:
TRAIN YOURSELF TO BE PRODUCTIVE

WHAT REGULAR TASKS CAN YOU BATCH?

WHAT DAYS CAN YOU BUILD A THEME AROUND? WHAT WILL YOUR THEMES BE ON WHICH DAYS?

Personal Branding Companion Workbook

master your time:
TRAIN YOURSELF TO BE PRODUCTIVE

WHAT ARE SOME OF THE TASKS THAT DRAIN YOU, OR STEAL YOUR PRODUCTIVITY? HOW CAN YOU AUTOMATE, OR OUTSOURCE THESE TASKS? WHAT TOOLS OR SYSTEM WILL YOU USE?

WHAT TASKS CAN YOU DELEGATE TO OTHERS? TO WHOM WILL YOU DELEGATE THEM?

master your time:
TRAIN YOURSELF TO BE PRODUCTIVE

WHERE HAVE YOU DABBLED IN THE PAST? WHAT CAN YOU BRING MORE FOCUS TO AT THIS POINT?

WHAT'S AN IDEAL WEEKLY PERSONAL BRANDING SCHEDULE YOU CAN KEEP?

Personal Branding Companion Workbook

master your time:
TRAIN YOURSELF TO BE PRODUCTIVE

WHO CAN JOIN YOUR ACCOUNTABILITY CIRCLE TO HELP YOU STAY ON TRACK WITH YOUR GOALS?

WHEN WILL YOU CHECK IN WITH EACH OTHER? WHAT TECHNOLOGY WILL YOU USE?

telling a true story:
UNDERSELLING YOURSELF, IMPOSTOR SYNDROME

WHAT AREAS DO YOU OFTEN HEAR THAT YOU ARE BEING TOO MODEST IN YOUR PERSONAL BRAND?

WHAT REMARKABLE PARTS OF YOUR WORK DO YOU TEND TO DOWNPLAY, OR HAVE YOU DOWNPLAYED IN THE PAST?

telling a true story:

UNDERSELLING YOURSELF, IMPOSTOR SYNDROME

WHAT MAJOR ACCOMPLISHMENTS CAN YOU REFERENCE MORE IN SELLING CONVERSATIONS?

WHAT CAREER WINS AND CASE STUDIES CAN YOU SHARE MORE AGGRESSIVELY TO LAND NEW OPPORTUNITIES?

telling a true story:
UNDERSELLING YOURSELF, IMPOSTOR SYNDROME

WHEN WAS THE LAST TIME YOU MADE A LIST OF YOUR ACCOMPLISHMENTS? MAKE A LIST NOW.

WHAT PAST ACCOMPLISHMENTS ARE YOU INTENTIONALLY DOWNPLAYING BECAUSE THEY HAPPENED LONG AGO?

Personal Branding Companion Workbook

telling a true story:
UNDERSELLING YOURSELF, IMPOSTOR SYNDROME

WHAT TEAM ACCOMPLISHMENTS COULD YOU STAND TO TAKE MORE CREDIT FOR?

IF IMPOSTOR SYNDROME IS AN ISSUE FOR YOU AND YOU OFTEN FEEL LIKE A FRAUD, LIST THE REASONS YOU THINK OTHERS MAY SEE YOU AS SUCCESSFUL.

telling a true story:
UNDERSELLING YOURSELF, IMPOSTOR SYNDROME

IN WHAT SITUATIONS DO YOU FIND YOURSELF SHRINKING OR LACKING YOUR NORMAL CONFIDENCE?

WHAT STEPS CAN YOU TAKE TO INCREMENTALLY BUILD YOUR CONFIDENCE IN THESE AREAS?

Personal Branding Companion Workbook

telling a true story:
UNDERSELLING YOURSELF, IMPOSTOR SYNDROME

HOW DO YOU ALLOW COMPARISON TO ROB YOU OF THE SATISFACTION AND FULFILLMENT YOU DESERVE?

telling a true story:

UNDERSELLING YOURSELF, IMPOSTOR SYNDROME

WHAT SELF-DEFEATING NEGATIVE MESSAGES DO YOU NEED TO CONFRONT IN ORDER TO MAKE YOURSELF MORE VISIBLE?

Personal Branding Companion Workbook

JOURNAL

JOURNAL

JOURNAL

JOURNAL

NOTES

NOTES

NOTES

NOTES

PLANS // TO DO

PLANS // TO DO

PLANS // TO DO

PLANS // TO DO

"It's time to share your genius with the world."

ABOUT THE AUTHOR

AMANDA MILLER LITTLEJOHN is an idea oven, brand problem solver, and creative powerhouse working at the intersection of public relations, journalism, marketing and social media. A former full-time print journalist and a writer first by training and passion, Amanda uses her unique storytelling lens and new media skills to help her clients uncover and subsequently share better brand stories.

A passionate teacher and trainer, Amanda is a motivating business coach for budding entrepreneurs and experts who are seeking brand clarity, new marketing perspectives, or fresh ideas on how to emerge as experts in their chosen fields. She helps people uncover their "unique genius" in order to share it with the world.

High achievers across the globe - from San Francisco to Saudi Arabia trust Amanda as their coach. Her clients have spanned industries - from government appointees to non profit leaders to academic researchers to CEOs. She has coached senior leaders and teams from corporations including Intel, JP Morgan, Scholastic, COTY/Cover Girl, Colgate-Palmolive, EY, WalMart, Guardian Life, Google, Spotify, TD Bank and Johnson & Johnson.

Amanda lives with her husband Marc and two sons in Washington, DC.

LEARN MORE

PACKAGE YOUR GENIUS 5 Steps to Build Your Most Powerful Personal Brand bit.ly/pygbook
PACKAGE YOUR GENIUS ACADEMY www.packageyourgeniusacademy.com
THE BRANDING BOX www.thebrandingbox.com
COACHING, MEDIA, AND SPEAKING www.amandamillerlittlejohn.com
CONSULTING, ETC. www.packageyourgenius.com

Made in the USA
Middletown, DE
19 January 2020